GW00502358

VW CAMPERS
Everything you want to know

Richard A Copping

SALMON

Introducing the VW Camper

If only it had been possible to predict 20 years ago what an old VW Camper would be worth now! Some of us would be millionaires; many of us didn't give them a second glance and compared to a Beetle they were cheap - merely geriatric, dusty and rusty!

Then everything changed. Not only was there a yearning for back-to-basics, the great outdoors and weekends away from the stress of the office or factory, but also nostalgia hit the big time. The oldest campers suddenly fit like a glove into the spirit of the age, their smiley front ends screamed retro and they were ideal transport for a snooze under the stars and riding the surf.

Easy to work on for the competent home mechanic, the underpowered aircooled engines were easy to ditch and replace with something a little more meaty, or if budgets were tight, rumour has it that an old VW engine never dies! Meanwhile, these Campers were an open book for home improvements — new retro units or the latest look, flower-power curtains and music to raise the roof. You could lower them or age them by adding traces of old sign writing, you might even create a little surface rust to get that sought after retro look.

It's all about camping!

With such a wealth of desirability at everyone's fingertips, inevitably prices started to rise and apparently even terminal rust buckets suddenly had a value. As the split screen examples of pre-1968 vintage attracted values out of the reach of many, attention turned to the second generation model, or the Bay as the panoramic windscreen model of the late 1960s and 1970s was nicknamed. The beauty of this vehicle is that it lends itself just as well to all the games people play with its older sibling. Inevitably, the second generation Camper started to increase in value too. Attention then turned to the third generation Camper, a product of the years 1979 to 1990. Recently there has been a growing following for the 'modern' watercooled T4, a vehicle only eclipsed by another incarnation as recently as March 2003.

The VW Camper Van has taken over the world. They are everywhere! You need to know more …

Sixty years of VW Campers in sixty significant points

Inevitably loaded towards the days when the Transporter was evolving from concept to a mainstay of Volkswagen's range, this rundown of all significant events in the Transporter's lengthy history makes an expert out of the novice Camper man

Large engine lid, 'barn door' – pre-March 1955

1) 1945 — Hitler and the Nazis are defeated and the Volkswagen Beetle factory is put into the hands of the British. Yorkshireman, Major Ivan Hirst takes charge.

2) 1946 — Hirst develops the *Plattenwagen*, or flat car, designed to move materials from one part of the Volkswagen factory to another. Using the chassis of the military version of the Beetle, the driver sits over the engine at the rear end of the vehicle. Dutchman, Ben Pon, a frequent visitor to the factory, sees the *Plattenwagen* and tries to arrange for its import to Holland. Defeated by bureaucracy, he soon has another idea!

3) 1947 — Ben Pon scribbles a sketch of a vehicle with a large load area, its engine over the rear wheels and the driver positioned over the front ones. Hirst takes Pon's ideas to his

Cab interior, single binnacle – pre-March 1955

superior officer. The inability of the Wolfsburg workforce to meet the demand for Beetles and a lack of manpower to rebuild the war-damaged factory results in a refusal to progress the idea.

4) 1947 – Ex-Opel director, Heinz Nordhoff, joins Volkswagen as Director General. He decrees that an economic delivery van of a totally different type than anything previously available will be built and sets his designers to work.

5) 1949 – Nordhoff increases the pressure after an initial van prototype based on the Beetle chassis collapses under the weight of the body, in April! A second prototype is ready for testing in mid-May. The new vehicle is launched to the press in November. Nordhoff advises that a whole range of options, including people carriers, pick-ups and even an ambulance, will be developed. He announces that the new vehicle weighs 875kg and can carry 850kg, thus creating a weight-to-load ratio of 1:1. The load area lies between the two axles.

6) 1950 – February sees a number of Transporters delivered to important customers, while in March, full scale production of the Delivery Van begins.

7) 1950 – In May, the Delivery Van vehicle is joined by the Kombi and the Micro Bus. The former has easily removable seats and can be used as a Delivery Van during the week and as a passenger carrier at weekends while the Micro Bus is the first true people carrier.

8) 1951 – In June, a Deluxe version of the Micro Bus makes its debut. With more shiny external trim, roof and upper rear quarter panel windows, and in most cases, a near full-length fold back canvas sunroof, plus a full length dashboard compared to the single instrument binnacle of other models, Nordhoff demonstrates that he plans to cater for the needs of all markets.

9) 1951 – Following an approach by a US officer to build a caravan style interior for a VW Transporter, the German coach-building firm of Westfalia goes on to produce a further 50 examples over the course of two years. They introduce their Camping Box for use in conjunction with the Kombi – essentially a series of self contained units that can be added at weekends and removed during the week.

10) 1951 – In December, a fully kitted out Ambulance is added to the list of official Transporter options.

Pre-March 1955 Micro Bus

1956 VW Ambulance

12) 1953 – The first engine upgrade occurs as a Christmas treat for Volkswagen Transporter fans as power is upgraded to 30PS from 25PS. Absurd as this may seem in an era of vans developing close to 200PS, the change was significant and in line with the offerings of other manufacturers.

13) 1954 – The 100,000th Transporter to be built since production began nearly five years earlier rolls of the Wolfsburg assembly line on 9th October.

14) 1955 – The Transporter is given an extensive makeover and on 1st March launches on a largely unsuspecting public. Key changes include: the provision of more adequate cab ventilation via air vents incorporated into a redesigned roof panel; a full length dashboard for all models; access to the rear of the vehicle and a practical loading platform via a hatch style door; reduction in size of both the cavernous engine compartment and its attendant overly large access door; relocation of the fuel filler cap from within the engine compartment to a more practical exterior location; repositioning of the spare wheel from the engine compartment to a site behind the front seat; and reduction in the size - but increase in the width - of the vehicle's wheels and tyres.

11) 1952 – The Pick-up is launched on 25th August. The design and press costs of creating a new much shorter roof panel, relocating the spare wheel to the cab, moving the petrol tank and developing the combination of a practical, low level loading bed and secure storage below that platform, are considerable.

The VW Pick-up with tarpaulin and bows

15) 1956 – Concerned that ever increasing Beetle production and the escalation in Transporter sales will result in the Wolfsburg factory being overwhelmed, Nordhoff announces that a factory will be built in Hanover for production of the commercial vehicle. The new plant kicks into action and the first vehicle, a Dove Blue Pick-up, leaves the premises on 8th March.

16) 1956 – The 13th September sees production of the 200,000th Transporter.

17) 1956 – Westfalia introduces a new full camper conversion known simply as the Deluxe Camping Equipment. Increased co-operation between Volkswagen and the coachbuilders results in the allocation of SO numbers – VW's special model designations.

18) 1956 – Austrian refugee, Peter Pitt, creates a modular 'Moto-Caravan' using the VW Transporter as the basis for his endeavours. Pitt proves instrumental in achieving the removal of legislative restrictions condemning the Camper to a maximum speed of 30mph. With its new official status as a motorised caravan, it is also exempt from purchase tax.

19) 1956 – Jack White, from the Devon resort of Sidmouth, oversees the transformation of his VW Delivery Van into a fully fledged camper for his own use on long trips to visit relatives in Germany. Such interest is shown in the vehicle that he decides to open a business producing his Caravette under the Devon brand name. 56 vehicles are sold in 1956 and the company goes on to become probably the best known name in British Camper conversions for many years to come.

20) 1958 – The emergence of many special bodied models with such diverse uses as mobile shops, hydraulic tipper trucks and even exhibition vehicles (mostly built by firms operating under license from Volkswagen) stimulates Wolfsburg to add a further model to the core range. Designed to transport up to six people, the Double Cab Pick-up offers secure storage under the new rear seat and retains the flexibility of the single cab Pick-up, Volkswagen's customers welcome the new model with open arms and nowhere more so than in America.

21) 1958 – Westfalia's Camping Box is revised and given the designation SO22, while later in the year, the full Camper conversion is similarly updated and allocated SO23. The American market starts to take the Westfalia Camper to heart.

Post-March 1955 – small rear window – US spec bumpers

22) **1959** – The 500,000th Transporter to be produced leaves Hanover on 25th August.

23) **1960** – Following a short period utilising a redesigned 30PS engine with a slightly higher compression ratio, in June, Nordhoff is able to announce the arrival of a 34PS engine, the extra power being achieved essentially through a new Solex carburettor.

24) **1961** – Another, and the last core model of the Transporter range, the High Roofed Delivery Van makes it entrance during September. Very much a case of 'what you see is what you get' – a storage space 14 inches higher than normal and a resultant height of over 66 inches – the latest option becomes popular with the likes of clothing firms wishing to transport full length dresses.

25) **1961** – Between 1961 and 1965 updated Westfalia models are given the designations SO34 and SO35. Both refer to full camper conversions, as do the numbers allocated to their 1965 – 1967 successors, the SO42 and SO44.

26) **1961** – With demand for campers in the USA far outstripping supply, Volkswagen of America turn to Sportsmobile, established RV converters, to produce kits which can be installed either by dealers or individuals. So similar in nature are these 'home-grown' kits that in later years wits nickname them 'Westfakias'! Within a short time, the generic name of Campmobile is established and covers both the homebred kits and Campers imported from Germany.

27) **1962** – Amidst a great deal of ceremony the one millionth Transporter, a top-of-the-range and heavily garlanded Micro Bus Deluxe, comes off the assembly line. Nordhoff makes one of his customary speeches in which he confirms that Hanover employs 20,000 people and 63 per cent of all Transporters are exported.

28) **1963** – From 7th January, US customers can specify a Transporter with a larger 42PS 1500 engine (essentially a bored out version of the 1200). From March, it is available with all passenger carrying vehicles, and from August, the full range. (From August 1965 as a result of larger inlet and exhaust valves and a new carburettor, the 1500 engine's power increases to 44PS.)

29) **1964** – Danbury Conversions produces its first camper conversion based on a 1963 model VW Transporter and names it the Multicar. Soon to become famous for the inherent simplicity of

1959–1961 Westfalia SO23 Camper

1965–1967 Westfalia SO42 Camper

their conversions, Danbury's heyday arrives during the lifespan of the second generation Transporter when for a time they are granted official Volkswagen approval.

30) 1966 – Six volt electrics are banished in August in favour of 12 volt.

31) 1967 – In July, production of the first generation Transporter comes to an end at Hanover with in excess of 1,833,000 having been built in the last 17½ years.

32) 1967 – A longer, wider and taller second generation Transporter is launched in August. All the options offered previously are immediately available with the new panoramic windscreen model, a vehicle which is soon given the nickname of the Bay. The second generation Transporter is powered by a 47PS 1600 engine.

33) 1968 – On 5th February, Heinz Nordhoff presents the two millionth Transporter, a Clipper (or Micro Bus) L to a German charity. Two months later the 69-year-old Director General dies and the future wellbeing of Volkswagen immediately becomes uncertain.

34) 1968 – On 8th March, Westfalia celebrate the arrival of the 30,000th Camper.

35) 1969 – August sees the Transporter fitted with stronger door frames and the stiffening of the four hoops which create the basis of the structure on which the body panels are lodged.

36) 1970 – In August, the 1600 engine acquires modified cylinder heads with twin inlet ports which allow it to breathe more easily. Output increases from 47PS to a maximum of 50PS at 4,000rpm.

37) 1971 – The 100,000th Camper conversion is completed by Westfalia. Daily production stands at 125. Export to the USA reach a new all-time high of 84 per cent of production.

38) 1971 – From August more than one engine option is available. The 1600 unit remains an option, while a 'new' 66PS 1700 engine (borrowed from Volkswagen largest aircooled saloon) is also offered.

39) 1971 – The 3rd September sees the three millionth Transporter roll off the Hanover assembly line.

Reasonably early 'Bay' Micro Bus Deluxe

Later 'Bay' with sturdier bumpers – in fire support vehicle mode

Brazilian built 'Bays' imported and converted by Danbury

40) 1972 – The second generation Transporter receives its only serious makeover of its production run in Germany. Most significant, although invisible, is the redesign of the cab floor to create a crumple zone. The bumpers are of a new reinforced design, the front indicators are relocated higher on the front of the vehicle and the external cab step ups are replaced with ones built into the interior of the Transporter. Primarily for the US market, Volkswagen introduces a three-speed automatic version.

41) 1973 – The first global oil crisis precipitates a drop in Westfalia sales of 35 per cent in the USA. The following year Volkswagen will make a loss of 555 million DM.

42) 1973 – August sees the 1700 engine discontinued and replaced by a 68PS 1800 unit.

43) 1975 – On 9th July, the four millionth Transporter leaves the Hanover assembly line.

44) 1975 – For the 1976 model year, which starts in August 1975, the Transporter is endowed with a 2.0 litre engine. The 1970cc 70PS engine is borrowed from the mid-engined sports car known as the VW Porsche 914.

45) 1979 – German production of the second generation Transporter ceases in the main at the end of July, although the last example of its type trickles off the assembly line in October. Amazingly, this is far from the end of the story of the second generation Transporter, as both Volkswagen's Mexican and Brazilian factories continue to produce it for many years to come. Latterly, production is restricted to Brazil, where a 1.4 litre 78PS fuel injected watercooled engine is fitted.

46) 1979 – Available for sale from August, the third generation Transporter, or T3, creates something of a furore. At a time when the old aircooled models have been swept away and replaced by front-engine, front wheel drive watercooled cars, the T3 emerges with its engine and driving wheels at the rear and is powered by 1.6 and 2.0 litre aircooled engines. Widely believed to have been sanctioned by Volkswagen's fourth Director General, Toni Schmücker, recent research indicates that it was the brainchild of his predecessor, Rudolph Leiding (1971–1975), who was the driving force behind the emergence of the VW Golf. The T3 is longer, wider and heavier than its predecessor. In the USA, the T3 is known as the Vanagon, a designation unique to this incarnation of the Transporter.

Air-cooled 'T3' – one grille equals no radiator!

Top of the range T3 with chrome and two tone paint

47) 1981 – The aircooled engines are supplemented by an in-line four cylinder watercooled diesel unit borrowed from the Golf. Developing 50PS, the diesel is no boy racer!

48) 1981 – September sees the launch at the Frankfurt Motor Show of the luxury seven seater Caravelle. Come August 1983, all people carriers are designated Caravelles. The workhorse models retain the Transporter moniker. In the USA, the highest specification models bear a Vanagon GL badge.

49) 1982 – New specially developed watercooled boxer engines replace the aircooled units in August. Both are 1.9 litre units – a single carburettor 60PS version and a twin carburettor 78PS offering. Each is quieter and more economical than its aircooled predecessor and as with the diesel can be identified as providing the vehicle's motive power through the inclusion of a second grille on the front of the T3 behind which lays the radiator. Later engine developments include a 70PS turbo diesel and a 2.1 litre, 112 PS watercooled unit.

50) 1983 – The luxury people carrier, the Caravelle Carat, is launched and is at first identifiable by its rectangular twin light housings. However, it isn't long before all North American bound models, even Pick-ups and Delivery Vans, are so endowed and by the final years of T3 production, this trend has extended to all European T3 models. From September 1985, the Carat becomes a standard part of the T3 range.

51) 1985 – After signing a contract in 1982 to develop a four wheel drive version of the T3, the Steyr-Daimler-Puch factory of Graz, Austria, begins production of syncro vehicles (the lower case 's' is intentional). Soon available as an option on all models, the permanent four wheel drive system involves a viscous coupling which facilitates transfer of power from the rear to the front wheels if loss of traction is encountered. The syncro system demands a new subframe structure at the front of the vehicle which in turn leads to the relocation of both the petrol tank and the spare wheel. The syncro system is mated to a four-speed gearbox which benefits from an additional cross-country or off-road gear.

52) 1985 – In September, Volkswagen debuts the Multivan concept at the Frankfurt Motor Show. Described as a vehicle that 'closes the working week and the weekend'. Rudimentary sleeping and dining facilities plus an icebox are included in what is otherwise a comfortable people carrier.

Double Cab Pick-up syncro 4WD

The conventional T4 1999–2003 in camper guise

53) 1986 – On15th January, the six millionth Transporter/Caravelle rolls off the Hanover assembly line.

54) 1990 – In July, mainstream T3 production ceases at Hanover in anticipation of the new T4 which is to debut in August.

However, syncro production continues until September 1992, the final vehicles being presented as a Limited Last Edition with each vehicle numbered as one of 2,500 such vehicles.

55) 1990 – Production of the entirely conventional front wheel drive, front located and transversely mounted engine, T4 begins in January 1990. Available in either short or long wheelbase form and with chassis cabs rather than Volkswagen's classic Pick-up arrangement, both the popular double cab and the high roof Delivery Van options are absent from the launch line up. A range of diesel and petrol engines offer between 61PS for the workhorse option oil burner and 110PS for a five cylinder petrol offering capable of 110mph.

56) 1997 – The bonnet of the Caravelle and Multivan models are made longer, partly to house a new VR6 engine option, but also in conjunction with moulded, foam filled bumpers to offer a more aesthetically pleasing appearance. The six-cylinder narrow angle 'V' (originally developed for the Passat syncro) develops 140PS at 4,500rpm. Transporters retain the original look. A top of the range Caravelle Limousine with VR6 engine, automatic box and such attributes as leather upholstery and full air conditioning costs twice as much as a two door Golf GTI.

The T4 with extended bonnet for the larger engine – see headlight shape!

The T5 in 2003–2009 guise 'dressed' as an ambulance

57) 2003 – Volkswagen launches the T5 in March with a vast range of options. Turbo charged diesels dominate the engine line up and all of which are endowed with *Pumpe Düse*, unit injector, technology. Although the range encompasses everything from an 1896cc engine developing 84PS to a 2460cc unit offering 174PS, considerable emphasis is placed on the latest four wheel drive models now branded as 4MOTION and a six forward ratio automatic box described as Tiptronic.

58) 2004 – Following the acquisition of Westfalia by Volkswagen's rivals, the Daimler/Chrysler/Mercedes-Benz group, a new factory is set up at Hanover to build the first full factory-designed and produced Camper.

59) 2004 – The landmark achievement of the ten millionth 'Transporter' is realised on 22nd September.

60) 2009 – A visually revised T5 with a front grille and headlights similar in style to those of Volkswagen's latest passenger cars is launched. PD technology is replaced by common rail TDI engines which offer both lower emissions and better fuel economy. All are 2.0 litre four cylinder engines and offer between 84PS and 180PS.

The Spotters guide to VW Campers 1950 to 1992

Fifty fast facts to help you identify what year the Transporter you are looking at belongs too. Health warning – serious headaches can be expected when trying to identify the birth-date of a customised 'Bus'!

1) If it's really old and has a massive engine compartment lid taking up two-thirds of the rear of the vehicle, it dates from before March 1955 and in enthusiast parlance is known as a Barn Door model.

2) If it's really old, has no rear window and a massive VW roundel on its rear panel, it's worth a fortune as it was built before 11th November 1950.

3) If it has got a rear window – assuming someone hasn't added it later, the vehicle has to date from April 1951 or later.

4) What if it's really old – big engine lid etc – and lacks a rear bumper? You are looking at a Delivery Van, Kombi or Micro Bus built before 21st December 1953.

5) Assuming the engine lid is of the Barn Door variety and the vehicle has 23 windows, including eight roof panel skylights, and curved glass in each upper rear quarter panel, you are looking at a Micro Bus Deluxe dating from June 1951 to March 1955.

6) Look at the front of the vehicle for a peak above the windows. Check the size of the engine compartment lid – certainly not covering more than a third of the rear of the vehicle. Peer inside and see if the dashboard is of the full length variety. Yes, on all counts – the Transporter dates from after March 1955.

7) Does the vehicle have the characteristics described in the point above, but the same delicate bumpers of all the Barn Door models you've been looking at? If so, it dates from March 1955 to August 1958.

Post-1953 Barn Door with ultra rare opening rear window!

23 windows – it's a pre-August 1963 Micro Bus Deluxe!

8) If the vehicle has semaphore indicators, it dates from before June 1961 – allegedly! Unfortunately, if it's an American market import, it will have bullet style flashing indicators above and outward from the headlamps if it dates from after April 1955.

9) Is the Transporter you are looking at fitted with towel rails? This delightful enthusiast term, refers to the two tier bumpers linked by substantial over-riders fitted to USA models from August 1958. (The upper bumper rail is much more delicate than the lower one – hence the towel rail appendage.) Beware, as they looked good, towel rails became a popular accessory on European market models.

10) Has the Transporter got some or all of the characteristics described in the last few 'pointers', but includes comparatively large sectioned rear lights? If it has these fittings it dates to after July 1961.

11) Look on the dashboard for an original equipment fuel gauge. They were added to the package of all vehicles from July 1961.

12) Starting in July 1961, North American Transporters featured larger, flatter front indicators. The appearance of these lights led enthusiasts to nickname them as 'fish-eye' lenses.

13) Fast forward to European specification Transporters built during or after August 1963. They lose the bullet style indicators and gain the US 'fish eyes'.

14) Look at the front and rear wheel arches. If they are of a reasonable size with a protruding lip, the vehicle dates from July 1962 or later.

15) A counting exercise. If the Transporter you are looking at has nine outward facing air vents towards its rear then it's a pre-March 1963 model. If Mr Health and Safety had deemed that the vents must face inward, and the rules said there must be ten of them, it's a post-March 1963 model.

16) Peer inside a Micro Bus and look at the headlining. If it's made from wool, it dates from before April 1963. If vinyl is in place, it's a later model.

17) The size of the rear window was increased in a similarly enlarged tailgate with effect from August 1963.

Bullet style indicators and towel rail bumpers – 2-in-1!

'Fish eyes' on a 1964 Camper from Canterbury Pitt

To confuse – Australian vents are high on the vehicle!

18) A Micro Bus Deluxe dating from August 1963 or after has 21 windows instead of the 23 counted earlier. The larger tailgate results in the loss of the curved upper rear quarter-panel glass.

19) Can you judge whether a wheel measures 14" or 15"? You need to be able to if you are to confirm that the Transporter you are looking at dates from after August 1963 – assuming you can't check the rear window!

20) From August 1965, the Pick-up had a larger rear window. The cooling louvres altered from eight outward facing ones in the rear quarter panel to nine inward facing ones over the rear wheel arch.

21) Now identify a Brazilian built Transporter that looks like a first generation Transporter but dates from the period after German manufacture had ceased to 1975. The most likely model to be seen is right hand drive (because it originates from South Africa) has the multifarious windows of a Micro Bus Deluxe, but not the skylights, and a near Kombi like interior.

22) An early second generation Transporter, August 1967 onwards, is characterised by: front indicators set close to the bumper of the vehicle, 'nice' curvy bumpers, a dominantly large VW roundel on the front of the vehicle and exterior cab steps.

23) When is a Micro Bus Deluxe really a Micro Bus Deluxe? When it has chromed horizontal window bars across the rear windows. But were they compulsory? Ah! Score an extra point if you speak authoritatively using the enthusiast term 'jail bars'.

24) The most reliable way to identify an early second generation top of the range Micro Bus Deluxe is by: a chromed VW roundel up front, bright-work surround to each window, trim round the front panel air intake grille, rubber trim on the bumpers, two-tone paint – the roof panel to the gutters being white. As a bonus, but not guaranteed, an all metal sunroof.

25) The Bay identification game requires players to delve into the minutia of year by year changes. If it is an American specification Transporter the unique-to-that-market side reflectors changed from circular to square in August 1969.

26) If the Transporter you are looking at has a black dash rather than one at least partly painted in the body colour of the vehicle, it's a post-August 1969 model.

An early Bay is characterised by ..

Post-August 1970 – look at the wheels. This one is from South Africa – the colour is authentic and it's Marina Blue!

What year – curvy bumpers and larger rear lights?

27) Five stud wheels were replaced by four-stud versions on all models from August 1970. All Transporters now bear flat rather domed hubcaps. The elongated ventilation slots of old in each wheel were replaced by a series of much smaller punched holes in the rim.

28) From August 1971, the Micro Bus Deluxe roof colour extends to what might be loosely termed as the waist or a point below the windows.

29) The 1972 model year Transporter is unique and therefore easy to identify. Look for old curvy bumpers, external cab steps etc, and modern many holed wheels, but with substantially larger vents in the upper rear quarter panels and large rectangular rear-light clusters.

30) Post-August 1972 Transporters, or 1973 models and beyond, have three significant visual/practical attributes. The bumpers of all models are now of sectional girder style. The front indicators have moved and are now at either end of the frontal air intake. The VW roundel is much smaller than previously.

31) From August 1973, and the 1974 model year, the petrol cap is no longer covered by a flap built into the bodywork.

32) Micro Bus Deluxe models of post-August 1974 vintage feature a narrow bright-work trim strip that aligns with the door handles and even the petrol filler cap.

33) A sign of the times – recession, depression 1970s time. From August 1974, the engine lid handle and boot handle are of black plastic.

34) A rarity dating from June to November 1978. You are looking for something that resembles a Micro Bus Deluxe, but features silver paint and Marine Blue cloth upholstery. This is a special edition model known as 'The Silver Fish'.

35) Spot a vehicle with the look of a first generation Transporter at the side and rear, but a second generation front, with no external cab step-ups and truncated rounded bumpers. It's a Brazilian second generation model built before 1997. (Very rare on UK shores!)

Girder bumpers, high up indicators, smaller VW roundel – post-August 1972

36) Post-1997 Brazilian Transporters are imported by Camper conversion firm Danbury. Look for a raised roof-line, mouldings in the metal of the lower sections of the cab doors, rounded bumpers without the inclusion of cab step-ups etc. If what you are looking at dates from after November 2005, it will have a radiator cover perched at its front, although Danbury offer a circular cover which has been mocked up to look like a housing for a spare wheel.

37) Early third generation Transporters are easy to detect. If the vehicle has a single grille with the headlamps built in at either end, it is an air-cooled model, which narrows its production to between August 1979 and high summer of 1982 (almost – see below).

38) If the air-intake vents in the upper rear quarter panels are 'made' of plain painted metal, your early third generation model dates from before January 1981, when black plastic fittings were introduced.

39) If the bumpers of these models are chromed with black plastic end-caps and there is an abundance of bright-work trim, you are looking at a Bus L – the top of the range people carrier.

40) From early 1981, you can be confused, as some vehicles featured a second grille running two thirds of the way across the front of the vehicle – in line with the indicators and neatly above the bumper. Look for the identifying badge which will include a prominent 'D'.

41) A watercooled third generation Transporter has two grilles. Specific year identification isn't that easy. If it has metallic paint it's a later model, if the badge at the back indicates Caravelle it is slightly later but not necessarily much, if it sits higher off the ground or has moulded plastic bumpers or rectangular twin headlamps it's later or something special that can be easily identified!

42) The Caravelle Carat arrived in September 1985 as the top model. Apart from a decidedly plush interior, the Carat can be identified by rectangular halogen twin headlamps, a front spoiler, colour co-ordinated moulded plastic bumpers and trim surround, plus 6J x 14 light-alloy wheels with 205/70 R14 tyres.

43) Beware – US market Vanagons were fitted with the Carat's rectangular headlamps too and from a similar time, while towards the end of the 1980s, all models had both moulded bumpers and

Diesel or watercooled – the two grille clues

rectangular headlamps instead of the circular versions of the former and black painted metal girders of the patent workhorse of old.

44) The syncro means 1985 or later. Lettering on the vehicle is a big giveaway, but assuming there isn't any, check out the size of the gap between the wheels and body. If it's bigger than average and substantially so, it's a syncro.

45) Having identified what you think is a syncro, look for the petrol filler cap. If it is absent from its usual location close to the offside cab door you have virtual confirmation. To make sure, crawl or bend and peer under the front of the Transporter. The spare wheel should be absent. Check if it is tucked upright into the rear luggage compartment.

46) The T3 Multivan – metallic paint and through the windows the rudiments of a Camper, but not one overflowing with units. A raised digit plastic badge on the back helps.

47) The popular TriStar Double Cab Pick-up is a limited edition model which ran from February 1988 and onwards. Surviving examples usually feature branding decals, the now rather dubious 'bull-bars' and are endowed with syncro – see above!

48) Find a T4 (1990–2003), take a step back and announce that the vehicle you are looking at has a length of approximately 2,920mm if it has a short wheelbase and 3,320mm for its longer sibling.

49) There are two types of T4 – from the 1998 model year, T4s fitted with the latest option of a V6 engine featured a re-designed and necessarily lengthened bonnet coupled to colour coded foam filled bumpers. To identify the original and continuing model from the new version look at the headlights. The originals are virtually rectangles, while the adjoining grille is equally angular. The new model headlamps slope in at the top towards the centre, while the adjoining grille is gently curvaceous.

50) The T5 underwent a makeover in late 2009 bringing the styling of the front roughly into line with the house-look of the Mk6 Golf and the new Polo etc, etc.

T3 with rectangular headlamps – the Camper conversion is by Karmann

Fun with VW Camper facts and figures

Here are forty fascinating and fun-filled facts from the VW Camper files, all of which might prove useful if trying to impress at a gathering of like-minded enthusiasts

1) Enthusiasts have nicknames for the first three generations of Transporter. A model with a split pane front windscreen (1950–1967) is known as a Splitty, the second generation Transporter (1967–1979), with its panoramic windscreen, bears the nom de plume of the Bay, while somewhat disparagingly the T3 (1979–1990/92) is referred to as the Wedge.

2) Volkswagen expressed performance in metric horsepower or *Pferdestärken* (PS). To convert PS figures into British horsepower multiply by 0.986.

3) Nordhoff spoke of the Volkswagen Transporter when he announced the vehicle to the press and the name stuck.

4) The often heard name 'Bulli' is nothing more than an abbreviation of the words 'bus' as in *Kleinbus* (Micro Bus) and *Lieferwagen* (Delivery Van) with an additional 'l' inserted to bond the short forms together.

Home on wheels – pretty paint!

5) 1964 was the best year for first generation Transporter production when 187,947 vehicles rolled off the Hanover assembly line.

Fun on wheels – custom paint

6) The Delivery Van remained the most popular option through the first generation years. 48,481 such vehicles alone were built in 1964. Vying for second place were the Kombi and the Pick-up, the former achieving its best figure in 1966 with 46,284 units built and the latter 39,832 vehicles in 1964.

7) The Transporter's top speed with a 25PS engine was probably in the region of 55mph, although Volkswagen quoted 50mph as a natural limit. Acceleration between 25mph and 50mph stood at a sloth like 80 seconds. Petrol consumption varied between 30mpg at a steady 50mph to below 20mpg in areas of congestion.

8) The majority of brochures produced to promote the Transporter in the 1950s featured the highly collectable handiwork of artist, Bernd Reuters. His style was to exaggerate the length and curves of the vehicle, streamline its appearance, add 'speed' airflow lines, portray items such as wheels and seat backs as chunkier than reality, and include a disproportionately small driver and passengers to give illusions of space.

9) Many Delivery Vans, some Kombis and even Microbuses left Volkswagen wearing nothing more than a lick of primer. Why?

Looks good – 'period' lettering

Companies liked to apply their house livery.

10) More on paint – the near standard colour for the Delivery Van was blue. In the era of the first generation read 'Dove Blue', for the second think 'Neptune Blue' and with the third be bored by the blandness of 'Medium Blue'.

11) If you wish to become a paint colour identification expert, you are going to have to learn all about Campers too, for many a company re-sprayed a single colour van to offer a two tone effect. In later years – and here the reference is to the second generation Transporter – the roof and the panels to the waistline of the vehicle were often given a splash of white.

12) A Transporter endowed with the 30PS engine accomplished the 0–50mph sprint in 30.6 seconds and 0–60mph in 75 seconds.

13) The letters CKD stand for 'Completely Knocked Down' and refer to kits despatched from Wolfsburg or Hanover for assembly in one of Volkswagen's satellite factories. Local content was often restricted to items such as window glass and paint.

The primer look!

Deliberately polished away to give an aged look

In vogue 'rat look'

14) The most unusual, and undoubtedly the least successful Camper conversion dates from 1962, when Caraversions of London produced its HiTop. An enormous structure sat above the converted Kombi, making the vehicle decidedly unwieldy.

15) Initially employed to market the Beetle, the advertising agency DDB, Doyle Dane Bernbach, soon acquired the portfolio for the Transporter as well as creating a vast array of witty, one point adverts for both models. Cult status beckoned for the vehicles and automobile advertising was transformed forever.

16) Production of the first generation Transporter continued in Brazil until 1975 with between on average 25,000 to 45,000 units being built annually. Some were bought by Volkswagen of South Africa who marketed the first generation Transporter as the Fleetline, a budget model which ran alongside the new second generation Transporter.

17) Camper conversion firm, Devon, started life with its Caravette, but other names were added and withdrawn with frequent monotony. For example, during 1962, Devon added a no-frills Devonette to the range, which was replaced by the Torvette in 1965. With the advent of the second generation Transporter, a

Daily driver on garden centre duties

Still to be found in a barn

top-of-the-range Eurovette was added, but by 1970, it was all-change with a posh Moonraker and lighter duty Sunlander.

18) The second generation Transporter's windscreen was 27 per cent larger than the combined split screens of its predecessor.

19) Such was the demand for the second generation Transporter that the Emden factory was seconded to supplement Hanover's toils, concentrating on models for the US market.

20) The second generation Transporter currently holds the record for the highest annual production, an accolade achieved in 1972 when 259,101 vehicles were built.

21) The Hanover factory holds another record, as in 1973, it produced 234,788 Transporters on its own, a figure not as yet equalled.

22) 1970 saw the highest level of Transporter exports to the USA with 72,515 examples finding their way across the Atlantic.

23) The most popular model of second generation Transporter was the Kombi. In 1972, a total of 90,712 Kombis were built compared to 56,119 Delivery Vans. Micro Bus production also out-performed that of the Delivery Van on occasion. In 1971, its best year, 71,719 examples were manufactured compared to 47,913 Delivery Vans.

24) Total second generation Transporter production – excluding models produced after German manufacture ceased – stands at 2,465,000.

25) At launch, the second generation Micro Bus and Micro Bus Deluxe were branded as the Clipper and Clipper L respectively. The airline company, BOAC, objected as they had been running a Clipper Class of flights to the USA. With legal skirmishes mounting, Volkswagen beat a hasty retreat.

26) Unlike the all-metal first generation High Roof Delivery Van, the Bay version featured a fibreglass extended roof section with the intention of keeping the overall weight of the vehicle down.

27) The Dutch firm, Kemperink, produced long wheelbase versions of the Pick-up, which when completed looked more like a Delivery Van. They also produced an extended version of the Double Cab Pick-up. To achieve their aim they took a standard

Rare Camper from South Africa up for sale at an auto-jumble

Concours line-up – spit and polish please

A rare sight – making a few adjustments!

model and hacked their way through the platform area before inserting a 900mm extension.

28) From 1972, Westfalia attributed names to its Camper conversions to suit both the European and American markets. Hence, while there was a Luxembourg, a Helsinki and the Madrid, there was also a Los Angeles, a Houston and a Miami.

29) For a time Devon Campers sold a model named the Continental. This was nothing less than a RHD version of a Westfalia Camper – how bizarre!

30) Motorhomes – later Motorhomes International – introduced a Spacemaker elevating roof in 1974. This is one to look out for as when it is in the up position the structure overhangs the Transporter's near side making for exceptionally spacious upper floor sleeping accommodation.

31) The German firm of Tischer created a work of genius when they devised a separate 'camper room' that could be attached and detached to a workaday Pick-up with great ease. A Double Cab version was also available.

32) The 1700cc, 1800cc and 2.0 litre 'suitcase' engines were much flatter in their layout than earlier aircooled engines as all three had been designed to either sit under a luggage storage area as was the case with the VW 411/412, or in the middle of the car where the VW Porsche 914 was concerned.

33) Only the diehard enthusiast would argue that aircooled engines aren't heavy on petrol. Testing under the most favourable of conditions Volkswagen claimed an overall fuel consumption figure for the 2.0 litre engine of 23.0mpg. An independent tester achieved 22mpg overall on a series of journeys which included motorway travel. The 0–60mph sprint took 21 seconds.

34) T3 production numbers were consistently lower than those of the second generation Transporter. The best year was 1980 when a total of 217,876 vehicles were produced, and worst year was 1987 when numbers had fallen to 145,380.

35) According to Volkswagen of America, the creators of the name Vanagon, the word is simply a combination of 'van' and 'station wagon'.

Dormobile classic Camper

36) The first diesel engine for the Transporter, a 50PS unit borrowed from the Golf in 1981, was no earth-mover. 0–50mph times were quoted as being no better than 24.4 seconds when mated to a four speed gearbox, and 25.7 seconds when coupled to a five speed gearbox. Top speeds were 68mph and 64mph respectively.

37) The Joker was the name given to a Westfalia Camper conversion introduced at the time the T3 made its debut and a layout which survived until 1987 when it was superseded by the California and the Atlantic.

38) The American name for the fourth generation Transporter was the undoubtedly cringe-worthy 'EuroVan'.

39) A short wheelbase T4 had less available load space than the model it superseded, even though its overall length had increased, as had its wheelbase (5.4m³ compared to 5.7m³ for the T3).

40) The New Beetle started life as a design study in the USA and, once the decision had been taken to market it across the world, had its own healthy following. A similar retro design study which bore a passing resemblance to the first generation Transporter sadly didn't make it to production.

Late Split – subtle trimmings!

What's a VW Camper worth?

Just when as a non owner you have become truly enthused to buy your very first Camper, along comes some wise-guy to announce that a second mortgage might be required. However, as an owner already you give thanks to the worshipful author and confirm you have both a friend for life and an appreciating asset!

Let's be honest, first generation Campers or Transporters aren't particularly practical. Second generation models are much better, while later third generation models are positively modern! The charm of the first generation model is in its looks, its smiley face and its retro appeal, and that filters through to the second generation model. Whether it goes as far as the third is open to question. But old VWs wearing their original specification are both slow and thirsty, while six-volt electrics imply candle power lights. When mechanically modified it's a different ball game, and that's the beauty of owning an old though not necessarily 'antique' Volkswagen.

For all but the Concours kings and queens, the essence of owning a Camper and its desirability to others, even much of its inherent value, is in the tweaking; the personalisation which makes it a home on wheels and a part of the family. You might repaint it in your favourite colour; you could make it appear older than it really is by adding half faded out period artwork or lettering in the style of the decade during which it was born. You might opt to make it look rustier and more battered than it really is! Simply sand away some of the paintwork and let the elements do their best for a short period. Seal the 'damage' with oil or varnish and you have what is known as a 'rat look', and they have their own very definite following. You lower it, you add special wheels, you smooth out trim, replace light fittings, one hundred and one things to customise the exterior!

Whichever route you go down with the exterior, the interior has to work for you. Stereo, DVD player, highly polished surfaces, laminate flooring, pretty flowered curtains and a scatter of homely

Would you pay as much as the cost of a new family saloon or more?

cushions, bespoke and ultra luxurious leather upholstery, special material covers. The list is endless and as low budget orientated, or no expense spared, as you want. Above all, for all but those Concours perfectionists, where originality has its own altar, it becomes another room of the house and a part of the family.

Now the dilemma of purchase prices is more or less explained. Costs are simply a question of supply and demand really. VW Campers are in vogue; they have been for some time and show absolutely no sign of going off the boil. People want VW Campers and generally the older the better is the maxim. In original, pristine condition, a Camper is going to cost a fortune and similarly fully restored, it's worth a mint. In need of work but with bucket-loads of potential, it will still have a comely value and is going to cost to achieve what you want in the longer term.

Of course, as first generation prices escalated and are now roughly comparable in many an instance with those of brand new VW Golf GTIs, pressure built on the 1967 to 1979 models in terms of desirability, while affordability became more difficult. Some today can still be picked up for the price of a brand new run of the mill VW Polo, but others are fast approaching a decent VW Golf without GTI status. The knock-on process continues so

that decent third generation models are most definitely on the up. Even a rust bucket of this era has a value out of all comparison to now rarely seen and highly undesirable contemporary offerings from other manufacturers. Possibly a T4 is the best bet in both terms of affordability for the age of the vehicle, but even these Campers have their own devoted following with forums dedicated to their continuation and wellbeing. As for the T5, and sorry, Herr Volkswagen, buy a brand new one and it is going to set you back many, many thousands of pounds. It is very popular, make no mistake, but depreciation will be an issue for some time to come.

A final thought ...

A wonderful world of camaraderie exists as those already owning a VW Camper will know. There is a VW show to visit virtually every weekend from the early spring to late autumn. Go to Vanfest – Malvern, Worcestershire in September – and you can't move for vans. Go to Bus Types in April and it's like one big holiday camp for a long weekend. New shows spring up and attendance multiplies faster than a banker makes his bonuses. Clubs and forums abound, gift shop trinkets in their style attest to the VW Campers' universal appeal. Go for it, become a VW Camper enthusiast!

Classic VW camping – hot water, deep water – up to you!

Published in Great Britain by J. Salmon Ltd., Sevenoaks, Kent TN13 1BB
Telephone 01732 452381
Email enquiries@jsalmon.co.uk
Website www.jsalmon.co.uk

First impression 2011
Second impression 2011

ISBN 978-1-84640-296-8
Printed in China

Front cover photograph: Three of a kind – Campers from the mid 1960s
Back cover photograph: Two generations – Bay to the left, Splitty to the right